AF527512

MAHABHARATA STORIES

The Battle at Kurukshetra

Subhadra Sen Gupta

Om Books International

At the end of their exile, the Pandavas returned to Hastinapur and requested Dhritarashtra to give their kingdom of Indraprastha back to them.

Yudhishthira said to Dhritarashtra, "Your Majesty, we have obeyed your orders. We have lived in exile for thirteen years and in the final year your sons could not find us. Now we want to return to our kingdom."

Duryodhana and his brothers were not willing to give anything back. Duryodhana yelled at the Pandavas, “I will not return even an inch of land to you. It all belongs to my father!”

Hearing Duryodhana's reply, Yudhishthira said very sadly, "Your anger and greed will bring disaster to the family, Duryodhana. If you refuse us then there will be war. Is that what you want?"

Bhima stared angrily at Dhritarashtra and said, "You only support your sons, Your Majesty, and go against your dharma as a king. I knew you will betray us."

And Arjuna said, "I have not forgotten what happened at the dice game when you insulted Devi Draupadi. We will meet next on the battlefield of Kurukshetra."

The Pandavas and Kauravas began to prepare for war. Many kingdoms like Panchala, Kashi, Magadha and Chedi joined the Pandavas. While, Anga, Kekeya, Madra and Gandhara sided with the Kauravas.

Duryodhana and Arjuna went to the city of Dwarka to seek the support of the most powerful ruler–Lord Krishna. Krishna was sleeping when they arrived. Arjuna went and sat at Lord Krishna's feet and Duryodhana sat by his head.

When he woke up, Lord Krishna saw Arjuna first. He said, "I will help both of you. You can make your request as I saw you first. And Arjuna, I give you a choice. You can have my army or you can have me."

Arjuna said, "I only want your presence at Kurukshetra. I will do the fighting." And thus he chose his best friend Krishna. And Duryodhana was happy to get Dwarka's famous army.

Lord Krishna said to Arjuna, "However, there is a condition. My brother Balarama and I will not fight at Kurukshetra. He has already gone away on a pilgrimage." Arjuna was surprised and asked, "Then what will you do?" Lord Krishna smiled, "I will be your charioteer and I will help you win the battle."

On the first day of the battle the two armies stood facing each other. All the great kings and warriors were there, riding on chariots armed with bows and arrows. The foot soldiers were fitted with spears, swords and shields.

Arjuna stood on the chariot driven by Lord Krishna. He was at the head of the Pandava army. He looked across the battlefield towards the enemy and all he saw were his family members and gurus.

At the head of the Kaurava army was his great-grandfather Bhishma, a man he loved like a father, beside him stood his two gurus, Dronacharya and Kripacharya. His cousin Duryodhana and his other brothers were also there.

A broken-hearted Arjuna laid down his bow and said to Lord Krishna, "These warriors are not my enemies. They are my family and people whom I love and respect. Forgive me, Krishna, but I cannot fight and kill them."

To give courage to Arjuna, Lord Krishna spoke the immortal words that became the sacred text we call the Bhagavad Gita.